CLOTHING

by Robin Nelson

first step nonfiction

Lerner Publications · Minneapolis

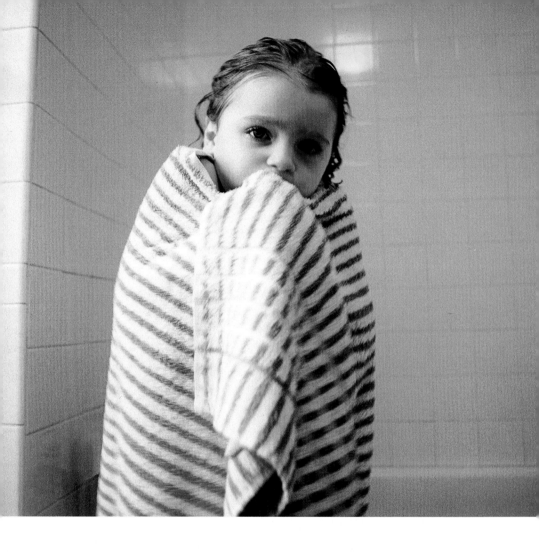

Everyone needs clothing.

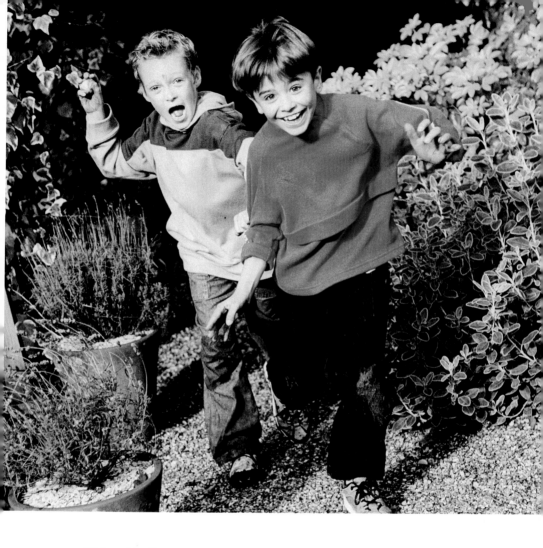

Clothing covers our body.

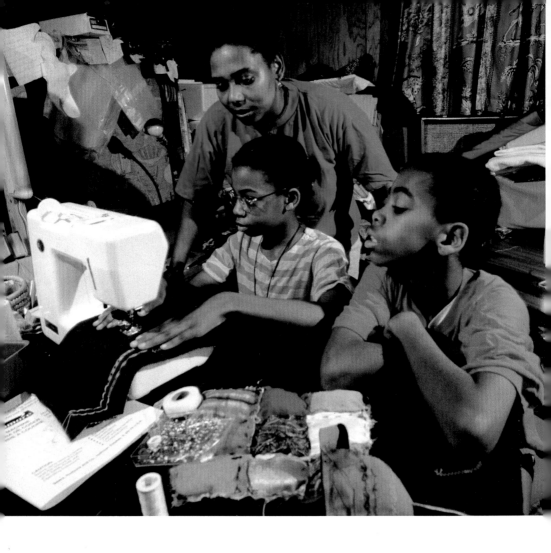

We make clothing.

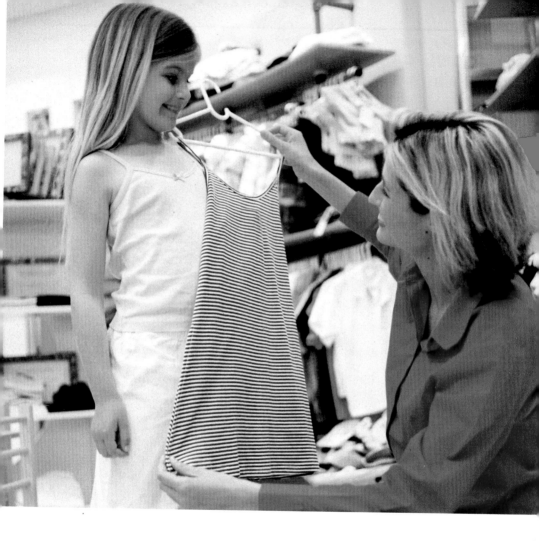

We buy clothing.

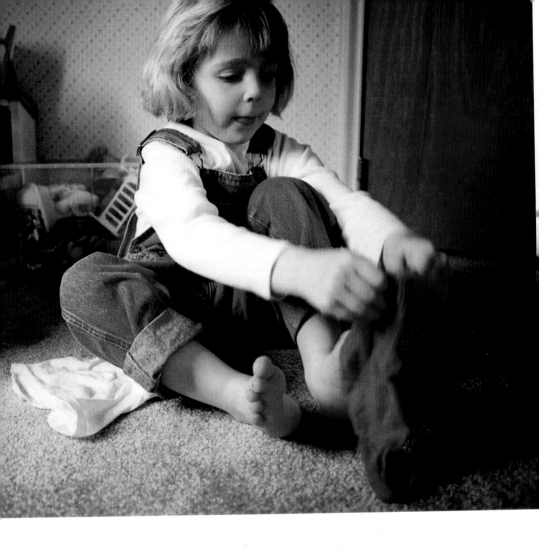

We wear clothing.

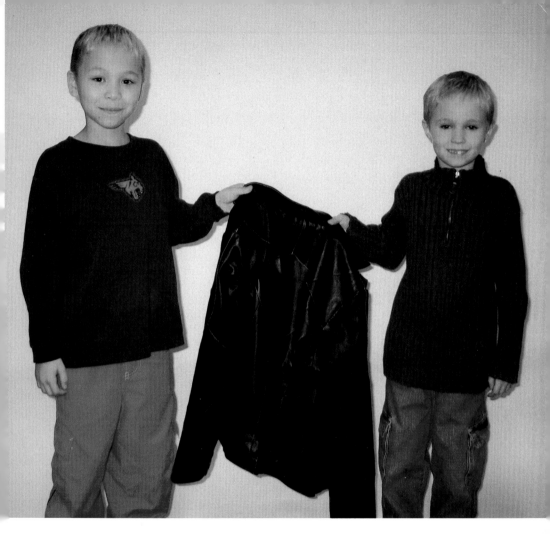

We share clothing.

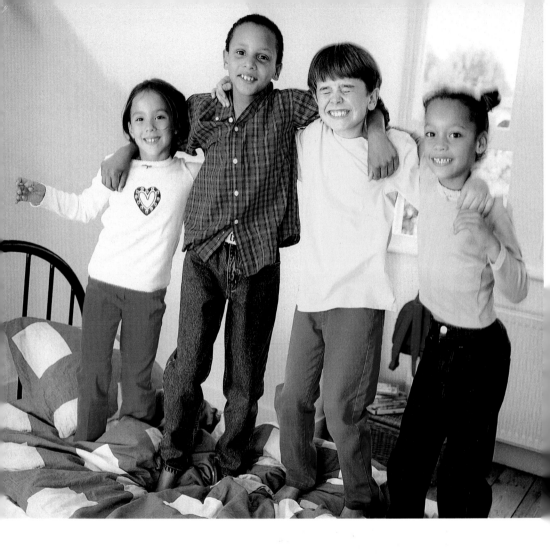

We all need clothing.